HOW I GOT 700 DATES IN ONE YEAR
II

(AND CONTINUE TO GET HUNDREDS OF DATES A YEAR)

By Mr. L. Rx

Revised and Expanded Edition – Includes Three New Techniques

Published by

Dating To Relating, Inc.

HOW I GOT 700 DATES IN ONE YEAR
II

(AND CONTINUE TO GET HUNDREDS OF DATES A YEAR)

Published by

Dating To Relating, Inc.
4001 Kennett Pike #134 - 590
Wilmington, DE 19807 USA

INDEX

http://www.DatingToRelating.com

BOOK I – The Original

http://www.DatingToRelating.com

Preface

Now with a title Like "<u>How I Got 700 Dates In One Year (and 2500</u> <u>Women's Phone numbers</u>)" it is easy for the point of this report to get lost.

The point of this report is not Mr. L. Rx bragging about his exploits, but quite the contrary.

The point of the report is to give men something relatively quick and easy that can help them meet and understand and relate to women better.

Yes, I went out on 700 dates in a year, but I did it because I was trying to learn about women and understand them and myself and male-female relationships better.

And the strangest thing happened to me in that year that I first did this. Simply by meeting that many women intensively I began to understand women better. And I began to recognize what they needed and wanted. And I began to get comfortable just being there with them.

You see, LEARNING is a natural thing. Given enough experience, we all will eventually learn. The problem with MOST guys is that they have never MET and DATED and RELATED to enough women to benefit from the natural learning process.

So you see the point isn't to go out on 700 DATES in a year for the hell of it, or to win bragging rights with the guys. The point is to go out on as many dates in as short a period of time as it takes you to kick in that NATURAL LEARNING process (called EXPERIENCE) so that you end up with your own NATURAL SELF TAUGHT understanding of women and how DATING and RELATING to women works FOR YOU.... It just happened to take me 700 DATES!

That is my intention in writing this report. I hope you can use it that way.

Good Luck

Mr. L. Rx

http://www.DatingToRelating.com

Ok, guys. Let me set the back drop.

I'm 40+ years old, I just got divorced, I'm a single dad raising two kids by myself.

I hadn't been with another woman in about 15 years (I'm completely faithful and monogamous when I am married) but it was time to get back into the dating game.

There were new development in the 90's –Voice mail, 900#s and personal ads for dating were proliferating.

With a sales background, although I was shy, I was attracted to "personal" ads in Newspapers. Seemed like it was direct and to the point and wouldn't require as much time as trying to meet women other ways….

A year later I had been on over 700 first dates and collected 2500 phone numbers. I am a little picky so I only went out with 3 women

7

more than once (my choice). One I ended up dating in a monogamous relationship for 7 years….

So now at the end of that 7 years, I'm almost 50 and I'm back at it again. But this time I was determined not to settle for less than my ideal mate. Even if it takes a lifetime to find her. So this time, I decided to use all my resources for meeting women -- personal ads, internet dating, dating services, friends, and hitting up on women on the street, in stores, etc.

Six months later, I was getting laid every night of the week by a different girl. I had 10 girlfriends from 22 to 35 years old and I was having a lot of fun…too much fun. So after a few months of that, I decided to slow down and only date about 4-6 girls and leave a few nights a week open to continue meeting new women and searching for my ideal mate.

Since that time, that has been my pattern. I am still searching for that ideal mate. I don't have time to meet 700 girls in one year anymore (That was 2 dates a day for over a year by the way - a part time job in

8

itself). So I have settled into having 4-6 friends, that I date and have sex with (a couple once a week each, a couple every other week or so, and a couple once a month or so.) I like to date and have sex about 3-4 times a week and I like to leave my other nights open to meet new women.

So in this mode I have been accumulating about 200-300 phone numbers a year and going on about 100 new dates a year for several years now.

http://www.DatingToRelating.com

ENTER THE DATING GURUS

So right about this time all these dating gurus start coming out of the wood work telling guys how to double their dating, how to get dates online etc. I buy these programs because I am always trying to improve my own game. After buying and reading a half dozen of these programs or so, I realized that my statistics are better than all of theirs. And although I can learn from these guys (there is always something to learn from anyone) I realized that there is a hell of a lot more that people could learn from me.

I even wrote one of the top "internet dating" gurus after I bought his program, and politely complained that after applying his techniques I was getting fewer responses than I was before. He responded that he would look at my profile and get back to me. Well after a couple of follow ups, he never did. It was then that I took a close look at his statistics that he so proudly announced to the world.

Yes he was going on 3 to 4 times the dates and collecting 3 to 4 times the telephone numbers that I was, but he had 50 times the

10

 http://www.DatingToRelating.com

profiles and sent out 10 times the emails that I was. Bottom line was pound for pound I was totally out-slugging him. No wonder my profile worked better than his.

HERE's HOW I DID IT and continue to do it.

MY DYNAMIC PRINCIPLES

I am trained in sales, so the core of my system is sales advertising technique.

GETTING SALES LEADS IN IS A NUMBERS GAME. The more doors you can knock on per unit of time, the more leads you have, the more hot leads you have, and the more closes you get.

Once you develop an ad that gets a response, the more newspapers you can get it in, the more leads you get, the more hot leads you get, and the more closes you get.

SALES involves three distinct actions, which require three different

11

technologies:

<u>DRIVING LEADS IN</u>

<u>QUALIFYING THOSE LEADS</u>

<u>SELLING THOSE QUALIFIED LEADS</u>

Now most people errantly think there is only one technology involved in sales. These people are bad salesmen, because they try to apply SALES TECHNOLOGY to UNQUALIFIED LEADS or the action of DRIVING IN LEADS and leave a lot of angry potential customers in their wake.

With the advent of PERSONAL ADS in the 90's and the legitimizing of INTERNET DATING in the 2000's getting masses of first dates is quite easy. BECAUSE YOU HAVE AUTOMATED TOOLS TO DO MOST OF THE GRUNT WORK FOR YOU.

Getting and going on 700 dates in a year was certainly a part time job. (It took about 4-6 hours a day of my time to do all the actions necessary to fulfill this) but without the automated tools it would have been impossible (unless I was a Rock Star) as it would have been a

http://www.DatingToRelating.com

FULL TIME job to do all the actions necessary to meet and date 700 women in a year meeting them on the street, through friends, etc.

NOW you can actually FORGET what all the INTERNET dating GURUS tell you about the content of your profile and emails. Of course some content is better than others and will get you a higher response rate. But for the first step don't even worry about that. The real secret is VOLUME of ADS.

Even the INTERNET DATING GURU whose program I bought admitted that he had 100s of profiles up while doing his research. He made it seem like the profiles were ONLY for the research, but in actuality it is the NUMBER of PROFILES that you have up that determines how many responses you get more than any other factor. AND it is simple, you don't even have to be good at writing profiles, just get a bunch of them up saying different things.

I first learned this when I was doing the personal ads in the 90's. I wrote a very conscientious ad put it in the newspaper and got 1 or 2 responses in a week. When I spoke to these girls and asked them

13

how their ads did, they would always say," I got 50 calls this week, or I got 100 calls this week, etc.

It didn't take me long to extrapolate from this that, as usual, in our society, GUYS approach GIRLS and very few GIRLS approach guys. BUT even so, there are a FEW GIRLS that do.

So realizing this I placed ads in 5 or 6 newspapers that carried personal ads. I got on the average 2 calls per ad per week. NO change there, but now, I was getting 10-12 calls per week. So then I started writing different ads. Stressing different things that I was looking for, or different qualities about me – you know things like SOUL MATE WANTED, then BEST FRIEND WANTED, then SINGLE DAD looking for SINGLE MOM, etc. (Actually keep your ads short. Usually the less you say in an ad the more calls you will get. Just communicate the theme in the title or heading and throw in a few other things – Here are some examples: SOUL MATE WANTED – I am spiritual, intelligent, and like physical activity. Looking for beautiful, sensual, partner. BEST FRIEND WANTED – Man. 6' 0", 165 lbs. Looking for beautiful woman –inside and out.)

14

Now then I only had about 5-6 papers available to me in my area, so I wrote about 4 different ads for each paper. So now – well you figure it – 6 newspapers x 4 ads each x 2 responses each = 48 RESPONSES per week WITH PHONE NUMBERS! (Actually it usually averaged just over 50.)

Now, being a good salesman, I knew better than to work RAW unqualified leads personally (Can waste a lot of time. Any good salesman wants pre-qualified leads) and the PERSONAL ADS were perfect because NO ONE could call me directly. They could only leave a voice message with a phone number and a description of themselves as I requested they do in my outgoing message.

So to qualify the raw leads I simply listened to the messages. I asked people to leave a message telling a little something about themselves and height, weight, nationality, etc.

The beauty about voice personals (As opposed to the internet) is you can hear the person's voice and message. This tells you a lot about

© 2009 Dating To Relating, Inc.   http://www.DatingToRelating.com

their personality. (Internet emails can hide a person's personality.) So bottom line is I used the voice messages to eliminate about half of the leads, then I called the other half. After talking to the girls, I would simply only go on dates with those that I could easily and effortlessly hold a conversation -- which worked out to be about 14-15 per week out of the remaining 24.

THE BEAUTY ABOUT THIS SYSTEM is you don't have to know any sophisticated technique. VOLUME of leads is what drives this system. YOU don't even have to be skilled at how to talk to women and what to say to women. I **guarantee** you if you just talk to 25 women a week on the phone, you figure out what to say in a very short period of time, even if you are SHY and UNCOMFORTABLE at first.

(I know this to be true because in my 20's when I first started developing VOLUME techniques, it took me about two months of meeting women before I got laid. I wasn't particularly smart at that time. I just kept doing it and slowly but surely the experience alone allowed me to figure things out.)

NOW same goes for meeting with 10-15 women a week. Even if you don't know what to do or say, the sheer volume of experience will enable you to learn naturally what to say and how to act, and to get comfortable sooner or later.

The personal ads I placed in Newspapers were free ads. Didn't cost me a dime. I had to use different phone numbers and names to place three or four ads in a newspaper, but most people have friends or buddies who will let them do that when you explain what you are doing. (If you want to pay for ads, then newspapers don't care how many ads you have and some free paper still don't care. I have 8 ads running at this moment in just one free newspaper.)

Note: Make sure you use Newspapers with some volume to them. If 2 women in the whole area are the only ones that read the ads, you are not going to get more than 2 responses no matter how many ads you place.

17

NOW INTERNET DATING is actually the same deal and same technique. A lot of internet services want to charge you for their dating service, but if you do a search there are tons of free ones — some of the best ones aren't free – but use what fits your budget. (Go to my website directory for the BEST and NEWEST ones to use: http://datingtorelating.com/online_dating_sites__directories_and_reviews Guys will usually get 0, 1 or 2 emails from girls a week by being totally passive—no emails out. So you are going to need 5 or 6 services and you are going to need to post 5 or 6 different profiles on each one to get any kind of volume (25-50 emails) in to you a week. If you want more or if your profiles are averaging "0" incoming emails (which can happen on some services) then you will need to email out about 250-500+ emails a week. (I usually average about a 10% response on emails to girls who are not a match – wrong age, etc. and 30% response rate from girls who are a match.)

MY PERCENTAGES are actually really irrelevant here. Because one of the basic sales principles is that it doesn't matter what your "close ratio" is, it only matters that you know what it is. In other words if your close ratio is "1 out of 3" or of it is "1 out of 100" you still have the

18

same ability to set goals and targets. The guy who is "1 out of 100" just has to work a little a harder to make the same kind of money as the guy who closes "1 out of 3." (And don't forget the VOLUME of your experience will cause you to learn things whether you like it or not. You may start out "1 out of 100" but that will improve as time goes by.)

SO THE POINT is that the figures I give you above, are my figures. The target you are shooting for is about 25-50 calls or 50/100 emails a week. SO SET UP however many profiles you need or use as many services as you need in order to hit those figures. Make sure you VARY your PROFILE content and HEADLINE content. I'd even use different pictures of yourself, so you are not obviously the same person. Different Women are attracted to different things. Six ads, all saying the same thing, won't help. Of course, there will be consistencies that you won't vary -- like age, height, weight, etc.

But STRESS different things about your personality in different profiles. In one you can stress that you like outdoor activities, in another stress that you like to read. In another stress that you are a romantic, etc. Get the idea? Also stress different female characteristics that you like in different ads.

Most importantly be real and be truthful in everything you say. I don't go into it a lot here, but ultimately it won't do you any good to attract women based on lies. You won't get very far down the relationship road if the attraction is based on lies. Experiment, keep statistics on which ads get the most responses. Change the unproductive ads. Try new things. Look at other guys' profiles on the service to get ideas.

If you don't know what to say or to email to these girls who email you or email you back at first, don't worry about it. (THIS is when one of those Internet Dating Guru books come in handy. If you have one use some of their ideas.) My most successful action has been to cut and paste a very simple response to a profile I like. Something simple like: **"Hi, I like your profile. Email me back if you would like to talk."** Again, I find the less you say the better. I've gotten 1000's of responses to that simple little email.

http://www.DatingToRelating.com

Whenever a girl emails me back, no matter what they say or ask, I simply go for the phone number. There are a lot of girls on these dating sites who are not serious, and are just there to kill time, amuse themselves, and flirt. DON'T PLAY THEIR GAME.

If they are seriously looking to meet guys, believe me, they will cough up the phone number. You just have to be polite and "in context." By "in context" I mean if a girl asks you a bunch of questions about yourself, don't respond with a simple "Can we talk on the phone?" PUT IT IN CONTEXT. I simply reply, "I would love to answer your questions, but unfortunately I don't have a lot of time on the computer. How about we talk on the phone. That will make it a lot easier for me."

So, no matter what they say or ask me, I politely come back at them (in context) with "Let's talk on the phone." Or "Would you like to talk on the phone?"

I never give them my number (doesn't work too good –unless they are Asian – And I mean Asian-Asian – not American-Asian.) And if

21

they don't give me their number, they DON'T QUALIFY. I simply drop the line. I don't re-email them, etc.

About a third to half the girls do give you their numbers and that is good enough for me, and will give you a good volume of dates each week. From there I work it just like I did with the voice personals.

And remember, if my statistics aren't the same as yours, the technique will still work. Just keep adding profiles and services until you get a nice flow of 25 - 50 phone numbers a week.

NOW THIS IS THE CORE yet simple TECHNIQUE that got me 700 dates in one year and maintains a flow of 100 dates or so a year since then (when I'm not in a relationship).

HOW DO THE TWO TECHNIQUES COMPARE?

Personally, I prefer VOICE PERSONAL ADS and EVEN NEWSPAPER INTERNET ADS over INTERNET DATING SITES almost on the order of 5 to 1.

WHY?

1) The girls on the internet dating sites are often just playing around, flirting, just window shopping, not serious. They waste a lot of my time. When I have a good Newspaper campaign going. I don't even bother to send out emails. I just answer the emails that girls send me on the Internet Dating Sites. Takes less time and it is more productive.

2) Most (about 95%) of the girls on the internet sites traditionally look a lot worse in person than their pictures. They always seem to put their best picture up, and never look as good as their pictures when you meet them. Believe it or not, the quality of girls that I meet from voice personal ads (as long as I qualify them first for height and

23

weight when I talk to them on the phone) on the average look a lot better than the girls whose pictures I have seen on the internet. – GO FIGURE THAT ONE!

3) Personal ads, just take less of my time. There is a higher response rate to my ads than on the internet and the girls who call are more serious.

4) Personal ads, usually produce leads with NO or little competition. The girls on the internet sites all have ADS up too. And remember girls can get 50 emails in a day and hot ones can get as much as several hundred in a day. The girls who call on the personal ads in newspapers usually don't have an ad up. They are simply browsing through the paper, see your ad, and make a spontaneous decision to call. Maybe they might call 2 or 3 ads, but you won't have competition from 50 other guys a day like the internet.

5) Finally I guess I like the Newspaper Personal Ads better because I've developed relationships and gotten laid a lot more from newspaper generated leads than internet generated leads and the

24

newspaper generated leads have taken 1/3 to 1/2 as much time to generate as the internet leads. So for the time spent, I am about 5 times more likely to get a relationship going or to get laid from Personal Ads in Newspapers than on the Internet dating Sites.

IN SUMMARY

What I have given you here is an easy to implement, simple to understand SYSTEM that is guaranteed to get you results.

DATING without VOLUME of leads can be a lot more complicated than this.

Let me go back to the SALES analogy again.

VOLUME of LEADS is a salesman's most basic friend. If he can get a volume of leads most anyone can figure out what to do from there over time. Not everyone has equal closing ability. With a VOLUME of leads some guys may only close 1 out of 1000. Another may close 1 out of 100. Another may close 9 out of 10.

In the beginning, it doesn't matter what your "close" ratio is. Maybe it is 1 out of 1000. So use my techniques and generate 2500 phone numbers in a year and by the end of the year, with this scenario, you'll have 2.5 girlfriends. You see, VOLUME is workable no matter how bad you are.

Now for those guys who want to be PROS. Who want to learn how to be able to close 9 out 10 qualified women that they meet for a sexual relationship. YES you are going to have to learn a little more than what I have taught you here.

The techniques I have given you here are going to put you on the road to success. Some of you, once on the road, will figure everything out on your own. This is all you will ever need. Others will need additional help along the way to be ultimately able to close 9 out of 10 women that they meet. (Still others will have the ability to figure it out, but decide-- "Why bother, when someone else has already figured it out and is willing to tell me.")

That is why I have the book DATING TO RELATING – it goes into minute specifics and details and is the ultimate manual for guys who want to:

27

1) Take it to the next level and close 9 out of 10 qualified women that they meet.

2) Be able to pick up women in bars, in clubs, on the street.

3) Be able to seduce a woman—any woman, that has absolutely NO INTEREST in you.

4) To be able to make love to your woman like no other man has ever done it.

5) To be able to meet and keep a hot woman that you are totally in love with for the rest of your life.

Yes, you can learn how to do all of these things, too. But I digress.

There is still more to learn about how I got 700 dates in one year because since then, I have maintained 100s of dates a year with casual effort and have come up with more new and exciting ways to meet 100s of women a year.

Book II –

Maintenance and New Techniques

http://www.DatingToRelating.com

Maintenance – How To Maintain 100 Dates A Year

Well to maintain a 100 dates a year, you don't have to be quite as aggressive. You can narrow your ads down to the most efficient ones, the ones with the best leads, and the most time effective.

I maintain 100 dates a year with a few ads on a few sites like backpage.com, craigslist.org match.com and friendfinder.com.

But you should do the whole gamut of sites first to see which ones work best for you and get you the quality of dates you are looking for.

In addition you may want to use some of the new techniques I outline in book two, as they can pull in more targeted and higher quality of women.

Personally, I now chose to meet about 2-4 highly targeted women a week rather than 2 a day.

Scam profiles have been a real problem for a few years now.

What are scam profiles?

Scam profiles are profiles posted by sex sites and con artists who simply want to part you from your money.

Scam profiles began with the sex sites trying to con you into signing up for a sex site on the internet, then moved into the "Nigerian" and Russian scams that try to bilk men out of money.

Their mode of operation is simple. They simply post pictures and profiles of hot young women (sometimes older women) and then wait to be contacted or contact men directly. (By the way the pictures usually aren't even real. More than likely you are being contacted by a little old man in Russia who has used the picture of a hired model to put up a profile to scam you with.)

31

The first "sex scams" were simple. They would send you a simple email sort of like this:

> Hi there, I saw your profile on the site and honestly it was the only one I really liked. You seem really nice.
>
> I have some more pictures at www.mysite.com and they are kind of private. My girlfriends talked me into taking them. Anyway I only show them to people I really like. You may have to sign up to see them, but it is free so don't worry it won't cost you anything.
>
> Hope to hear from you soon.

When you visited her site, the pictures often looked like amateur sexy photos and then you were warned that there were some totally nude photos but you had to join this site to see them. Of course it is a porn site or a porn "cam" site and the whole idea is to get you to join.

There are a million variations on this scam and most of the time now girls are just more blatant about it and will often just say something like, "come see me be naughty on my cam".

After a while the "Nigerian" and "Russian" scams started appearing.

The Nigerian scam usually works like this:

There is a picture of a beautiful young woman on the site. You email her and she emails you back. She says that she likes your profile and that she would like to meet you but she is "out of the country" right now on a business trip. Usually the business trip is involving her "furniture" or antique business (but not always) and she is traveling in West Africa. (Or she is in Italy or some such country now, but ends up in West Africa as you continue to talk to her.) She says she will be back in about a week and would like to meet you.

She will email you back and forth for about a week saying nice things and how she really can't wait to meet you when she gets back.

Finally, before she gets back, a day or two before she is to come back and meet you, she will get robbed in her hotel room or have some such other unfortunate accident, and will cry to you in an email that she is stuck in West Africa with no money and no way to get home.

http://www.DatingToRelating.com

She will then come up with some help but be short anywhere from $200 to $600 to get her ticket home and ask you for help. If you are a sucker and stupid you will help her and never hear from her again.

Of course there are a million variations on the above scam.

The Russian scam is similar:

It starts with a picture of a beautiful young Russian lady who again falls totally in love with you over the internet and announces that she is planning a trip to the USA on a new visa program and can't wait to meet you. She will be coming to the US in a week or two.

She will write you back and forth each day and then she will tell you she is leaving her small Russian town to go to Moscow or some other big city where she will catch a plane to the US. Finally right before she is ready to leave she discovers she made a mistake and the train ride or something was more than she expected and she is about $200 to $600 short to get her ticket. She will ask for your help and promise to work for you or get a job in the US to pay you back.

34

Of course, if you send the money you will never hear from her again.

Now scams are pretty easy to spot once you know the above patterns. Just remember there are a million variations on the above themes. They will all ask you for money and usually a small amount that you won't mind parting with. But remember they are probably asking 100s of men to give them these small amounts each week.

OTHER ways to spot the scams:

- They are always beautiful women, with pictures that look professional rather than amateurish.
- They fall in love or "like" with you too quickly.
- Their emails are most often non sequitur. They have cut and paste responses that don't exactly respond to what you wrote. (The better con artist will write situationally appropriate emails however.)
- Their English will be odd or poor even though they claim to be American. (The Nigerians often use the word "mum" for mother for example.)
- They will use words like "god fearing" and "Christian."

Now these are the basic run-of-the-mill scams but some scams can get quite sophisticated and can bilk people out of thousands or tens of thousands of dollars.

http://www.DatingToRelating.com

Here are a few web sites you can go to for pictures and more descriptions of the latest scams:

http://www.datingnmore.com/fraud/scam_database.htm

http://scam.chanceforlove.com/

http://www.hoax-slayer.com/internet-dating-scams.shtml

http://www.stop-scammers.com/

To get more information on "Dating Scams" just do a Google search for "dating scams".

REMEMBER never give anyone you meet on dating sites any money.

http://www.DatingToRelating.com

New Techniques – Non-Personal Ad Classified Approach

Now this is one of my best techniques ever as it is really targeted marketing, and there is NO competition.

Now the basis behind this technique is just meeting hundreds of women by placing classified ads in non-personal columns. Then interviewing these women. What kind of ads? What kinds of columns? Well I have placed ads in classified categories like:

Dancers wanted
Musicians wanted
Singers wanted
Actors wanted
Songwriters wanted
Secretary wanted
Nanny wanted
Assistant wanted

Now to be ethical about this you should only place a real ad for something you really want or need.

One of my best ads was simply:

Male 6'0 170 lbs looking for dancing partner to practice once a week.

37

I placed this ad in a column for "artists" "arts" etc. in a daily newspaper. What was really good about it is that women love men who like to dance and I really like to dance. So I had absolutely NO competition as it was not a "dating ad." But none the less it lead to lots of dates and lots of sex!

Another ad that was very successful for me was:

Songwriter looking for female singer.

I placed this ad in a column for musicians who are looking to meet other musicians. I played guitar and wrote songs, so I got to meet plenty of women with whom I had a lot in common, which of course led to other things.

Once I got totally sexual women by placing the following ad in a column where actors can meet and partner up to practice scripts with other actors. My ad said:

Actor looking for female actress to practice erotic script with.

When the girls called (and they did) I simply told them I had a chance to be in a friend's movie but it required nudity and fake sex and stuff and that I wanted to do it but I was really uncomfortable doing that because I was shy. So I needed to practice the script to get comfortable with the role.

Believe it or not I got a few very cute volunteers and easy sex.

Then there are the business ads. When I needed secretaries or nannies or some such employee that was typically a female job, I simply placed an ad and interviewed hundreds of women over several days.

I never came onto anyone, as I felt that would be inappropriate. Instead I simply let women come on to me. And if I liked them I was responsive.

The funny thing is if you interview several hundred women for a job, there are ALWAYS several that will come onto you.

39

Now overall this technique can be really easy, but it is targeted marketing and the only problem is finding a newspaper or online publication that has the exact type of classification that you want to run.

Just remember you are looking for a non-personal ad classification to run your ad in. Your goal is to 1) meet hundreds of women and let some of them hit up on you, or 2) to run a highly targeted ad that gets fewer responses but the responses are targeted for highly likely sexual contact with no competition - like the "dancing" ad or the "acting" ad.

New Techniques – Use Of Blogs

BLOGS – Girls Love BLOGS.

WHY?

Girls, women, want to get to know a guy. It is pretty hard doing it with emails. Emails just don't work that well. So a couple of months ago I started experimenting with BLOGS and simply saying when I contacted a girl on a dating site:

> "I like your profile and I'd like to get to know you better. Why don't you check out my blog. I write in it daily and if you read it you'll get to know me better."

Now, don't ALL go using the exact same words. You can say it many different ways.

Like:

> "Hi. Want to get to know me? Check out my blog. Make a comment if you dare."

OR

> "Hey. My name is Ron. You can check out my pictures and interests and thoughts at my weekly blog that I write. Make a comment if you are interested."

Get the idea. **Vary it.**

41

You see this is very safe for GIRLS. They can get to know you without any hassle. The conversions are great. BLOGS are real. EMAILS and PROFILES are static and really don't communicate who you are.

NOW that's the basics. And I'm going to give you some information on how to set up your blog for FREE. (In case you don't have one or the right type.)

You don't just want any blog. You want a WordPress blog. But you don't want a free blog at WordPress.com. You need a FREE BLOG on your own website.

WHY? Well it is complicated, but to simplify it, the WordPress blogs on your own site will get indexed in a few days and will also pull in random traffic from the search engines, so it is a lot more powerful than any other type of blog or website.

BUT THAT COSTS MONEY RIGHT?

http://www.DatingToRelating.com

NO!

I did my homework, guys. Get a FREE WEBSITE (no strings attached) with 250mb of storage, 100gb or bandwidth, NO ADS and Cpanel that allows even an amateur to set up a WordPress blog in minutes.

GET YOUR FREE WEBSITE HERE:

http://www.000webhost.com/50241.html

After you get your website. Set up your blog. It can be very simple. Nothing fancy needed.

POST a blog post every day for about 7 days (or if that is too much work, do one every couple of days but not less than 1 a week.)

You need a little bit of content so GIRLS can tell something about your personality before you start the next phase. Remember just BE

43

YOURSELF. You want to attract a girl who is attracted to who you really are – not someone else. So BE YOURSELF.

Post pictures or talk about your day, your job, what you think about girls, the troubles you've had with relationships, jokes, videos – whatever.

Now after you get some content in your blog. Post an AD or profile at the following FREE PERSONALS or DATING sites. And start emailing girls who post ads or profiles on the following FREE sites:

www.CraigsList.org
www.PlentyOfFish.com
www.DatingToRelating.net

and any other ones you can think of. Whenever you contact anyone, refer them to your blog as we did above.

Now this technique is very effective for meeting someone who REALLY likes you and who is REALLY compatible with you, but give it a little time. You need to get your posts up and keep them coming over time. It will start getting you action in the first few weeks, but it will work even better four months from now then it works it the first few weeks.

And don't be discouraged if you don't get a lot of action at first, this is a QUALITY technique – Go for quality rather than numbers. When someone does like you it is a good match because they took the time to get to know you and genuinely like you. GIRLS Like to get to know guys. The more posts you have over time and the more time your blog has been up, the more the GIRL feels she knows you and your statistics improve.

Remember this does not replace any of your usual ads. You do this in addition to whatever else you are doing and ask those women for their phone numbers as explained in the first book. This is best used for quality responses over time. This procedure pulls in a different type and quality of women.

45

New Techniques – The Letter Technique

So back to meeting women in volume.

I've gotten many letters from guys who have read "Dating To Relating" thanking me for giving them a technology that doesn't require that they have to be this macho, alpha male guy.

Well, that's true. You can be macho or not macho, alpha male or not alpha male. The "Dating to Relating" and " 700 Dates" technologies will still work.

A testimony of that is the SHY GUY routine I developed when I was about forty-five or so and still use. This is a really powerful technique as it can be used live in person, or on the internet, or by letters to random girls.

There are a lot of women who LIKE shy guys. So in this routine you simply be proactively shy.

46

http://www.DatingToRelating.com

The first time I used it, I was looking at a bunch of headshots and résumés that a producer friend of mine had on his desk. He probably had 500 headshots submitted to him for this project. As I looked at the pictures I was seeing hot girl after hot girl. The résumés even had an address and phone number. I asked him if I could have the pictures when he was done and he obligingly gave them to me a couple of months later.

I went through the 500 pictures and came up with 50 girls that I was really attracted to. (These were all hot young actresses that had auditioned for the part of a beautiful girl in a movie.) I decided that it was an awkward situation and I needed an approach that would be easily accepted by them. In other words I didn't want them to think I was a stalker. I finally decided that the best approach was I would write them a letter. The "Shy Guy" letter. It went like this:

Hi _____,

My name is Mr. L. Rx, and I must tell you that I find it extremely hard to write you this letter, as I am a rather shy person. But I recently saw your picture on the desk of a producer friend of mine and I was immediately stricken.

47

It was not just because you are beautiful, which you obviously are, it was something else that attracted me... I think it is the look in your eyes in that photo. They say the eyes are the gateway to the soul, and there was something in your eyes that immediately attracted me to you.

I don't know anything about you other than your picture. You may be married or have a boyfriend and if you do I apologize to both of you if this letter is inappropriate. In fact you will never hear from me again unless you willingly respond to this letter. But I felt I had to take a chance and write you this letter if there was even the slightest probability that I might be able to make a connection with you.

I have been shy all my life, and it hasn't gotten me very far with women. Like most people I just want to meet someone wonderful, but when I occasionally see someone that I think could be wonderful, I unfortunately find it difficult to say anything to them about it.... even in a letter.

So I guess you could say my letter to you is a brave attempt to be a new person...and not let someone I am very attracted to just walk on by.

Anyway that is my story. If you would be interested in meeting me at all, then please call me at 888-888-8888.

Yours respectfully,

Mr. L. Rx

I think I got about 15 phone calls to my 50 letters from some of the hottest women I had ever seen. I mean hot – 9's and 10's. About 3 of those 15 were married but just wanted to thank me for the letter and

48

encourage me to find the one I am looking for. The other 12 were single and I went out on dates with them all.

After the success of this letter, I started trying the same routine live and in person. You can use it in a club, or on the street, in a library or in a store. You can use it anywhere and it gets a real good response – As long as you do it right-- Just so happens that a lot of women LIKE shy guys and want to help them get over their fears. They will do anything to help – and I mean anything.

When I did the routine in person it went something like this.

> Excuse me, but (deep dramatic breath) …this is really hard to do, (nervous laugh) I am really a shy person… (slower breath)…. but I saw you from across the room over there and I am really quite taken…

> I mean….it's not just because you are beautiful, it's your look, and the way you dress, and there is just something about your smile and the look in your eyes….. You just look like a really nice person.

> ….(breathe) I'm probably scaring you, and you are probably married or have a boyfriend but I just had to say hello and see if there was any chance that I could get to meet you.

[Stop and wait for their reply]

Now I hardly ever get a bad response and about 30% of the time I get a real positive response from really hot 9 or 10 women.

If you use the rest of the "Dating To Relating – From A To Z" technology you can very easily turn this "Shy Guy" intro into a date or relationship.

This routine has to be done convincingly. You should do it with appropriate "shy" body language [nervously look down as you talk, stumble, stutter a little, etc.]

Probably best to be done by guys who are or were shy. If you are not really shy chances are you won't like the type of girl who responds to this and ultimately it won't work out for a relationship.

A variation of the theme (if you are not normally a shy guy and don't want to be known as one) is to use the "Shy Around You" routine. It would go like this:

50

Excuse me, but (deep dramatic breath) …this is really hard to do, (nervous laugh) I am not normally a shy person… (slower breath)….you can ask any of my buddies …..but when I see someone I am really attracted to, I get really shy. …. I saw you from across the room over there and I am really quite taken…etc.…

Problem with the live routine is you can't go to a club and do it on 30 women, you'd blow it.

This has to be convincing when you do it. So use it sparingly. Don't do it over and over at the same place.

And obviously if any of you choose to use the routine you have to Vary it and not copy my words word-for-word or it will become known as a routine and lose its effectiveness for all very quickly. So change it. Write it in your own words. It's the idea – not the exact words – that works here.

How else can you use this routine? Well be creative, any way you can get a list of names and pictures would be viable.

http://www.DatingToRelating.com

One idea is to make a list of all the women you like that you are too shy to talk to. Try to get at least 50 or 100 names together so you get responses. If you don't know that many then do it with as many as you have and keep doing it until you have done a 100 or so.

http://www.DatingToRelating.com

How To Get A Second Date

Ninety percent of the women I go out with on a first date (and most of these are blind dates) want to have a sexual relationship with me by the end of the date. So guys have asked me, "What is the biggest mistake guys make on the first date that prevents ever having a second date or developing a sexual relationship (rather than a friendship)?"

Well there are several mistakes a guy can make. Let me summarize them here then go into more detail.

MISTAKES ARE:

1) TALKING ABOUT YOURSELF TOO MUCH, TRYING TO BE INTERESTING INSTEAD OF INTERESTED.

2) NOT ASKING QUESTIONS AND NOT LISTENING ENOUGH.

3) FOCUSING TOO MUCH ON SEX-- either overtly or by innuendo.

4) NOT USING SUBTLETIES ENOUGH (What a woman understands)

5) NOT DEVELOPING SEXUAL FLOW OR INTEREST.

6) NOT CREATING FUTURE. (A relationship is ALL about FUTURE.)

The first mistake that most guys make is that they go on the first date and talk all about themselves, sort of strut around telling the girl that he's got this car, and he's got this job and he talks and talks and talks bragging about this and that trying to impress the girl that he is a good catch.

What a girl sees is a self-centered egomaniac that isn't going to be able to take care of her at all, because he is not interested in her and doesn't listen to what she has to say. Not a good relationship prospect.

Another way of saying it is that guys try to be interesting. They figure they have to be interesting for a girl to be interested in them. Sorry guys, but it doesn't work that way. You have to be INTERESTED in the girl, not INTERESTING to get her attention. Did you ever see two interesting people on a date? It is hilarious! They are both so busy trying to be interesting to the other that neither has time to be interested in the other.

If you don't know what I am talking about, think what makes you feel better. A girl who is INTERESTED in you? Or a girl who is telling you

54

how cool she is, how hot she is, etc. and all kinds of other INTERESTING things.

INTERESTING leads to a lot of rejection and "platonic" friendships by the way. Girls will be friends with a guy who is really interesting. Why? Girls like to be amused and entertained. Interesting men are sort of like children to them. A source of non-sexual amusement and pleasure.

Then there are the guys who are SCARED S***less and don't know what to say. So they say all kinds of useless and banal and irrelevant stuff to again be INTERESTING to the girl.

Then there are guys who dread silence. So whenever there is a silent moment they feel awkward and have to fill the silence with some noise, so they open their mouths and say something trite and banal again just to keep the conversation going and again to be INTERESTING to the girl - THEY AREN'T. You don't have to fill silence with verbal chatter. Maybe it is a good time for some non-verbal communication -- like a smile, or a light touch.

90% of the girls I have a first date with want to go out with me again and have a relationship with me. WHY, well the biggest factor is I am INTERESTED in getting to know them. So I never come scripted, I am always just there and I ask questions designed to get to know the person in front of me. THE SECRET: Well, I just said part of it, so here is all of it.

I AM INTERESTED. I ASK QUESTIONS and then I LISTEN TO THE ANSWERS. Based on the answer they give, I may ask another question or I might say something that I know they would be interested in knowing because of what they just said.

MOST of the time I spend about 80% of my time on a date LISTENING. Girls like that.

ANOTHER BIG MISTAKE GUYS MAKE that prevents a second date is putting too much conversation attention on sex, sexual topics, sexual innuendos, and her looks.

ALL WOMEN THINK that ALL GUYS JUST WANT SEX. So basically, they are right and guys have to realize that girls have our number and are not impressed by it. GIRLS already KNOW you want sex. She

56

wouldn't even be there on the first date, if she weren't vaguely OK with the concept of having sex with you. What she wants to know is: WHAT ELSE do you want? What ELSE do you like about her? What ELSE can you do for her? What ELSE do you have in common with Her? How ELSE can you have fun together?

So, LISTEN to what she talks about, because if you listen you will get clues.

GIRLS communicate in SUBTLETIES and like to be communicated to with SUBTLETIES.

As a rule I NEVER tell a good-looking woman she is good-looking until the 3rd or 4th date. That is a subtle communication that tells her that I am not like all the other guys who kiss her behind.

So, you see, you don't have to tell a woman how pretty she is on a first date. (Especially if she is gorgeous, because she gets so much of this so often, it actually becomes a turn-off to her.) You can compliment her on her dress, or her shoes, or you can say she has a nice personality (find something non-sexual you like about her and compliment it) or you could say (but only once and non-repetitively)

57

she has pretty eyes, or a cute nose, or a nice smile, or she has pretty hands. (Always pick a non-sexual part of the body to compliment.)

So if you don't talk about yourself and sex, what DO you talk about? Talk about whatever the girl wants to talk about. LISTEN, and base your conversation off of what she is interested in. Ask questions about her. BUT you should have two goals for the night....

1) DEVELOPING SEXUAL FLOW OR INTEREST.

Now you don't want to TALK about SEXUAL stuff too much, but that does not mean you don't want to get the old sexual juices going. BUT you do that mostly non-verbally, not verbally (Unless she starts a sexual conversation with you.) Now some of the DATING GURUS have real good courses on how a man can be sexy and get a woman's attention sexually. (David DeAngelo's course comes to mind.) So let's just say it is done with posture, manners, attitude, movement, voice rhythms, and the occasional moving in close and the withdrawing, or light touch or holding of the hand momentarily. Verbally it is done with the right gradient of topic. If you do it right the woman will always give you a goodnight kiss as a further way of testing that sector out, and let you know by her non-verbal signals,

58

whether you should continue or just let it go with a simple light kiss.

It is better to develop it, make the woman want more, and walk away than to over reach and destroy everything else you have built up here. A simple hug, or a light kiss on the cheek or the mouth is what I do on 90% of my first dates that I am interested in.

2) CREATE FUTURE

What is future? Well if you are going to have a relationship with someone, rather than just a one-date-goodbye. You have to have some future interaction. AND FUTURE IS NOT "Can we go out again sometime?" That is definitely NOT FUTURE. That is a plea! Begging! And this will definitely scare them away. (Watch "Blind Date" on TV some time.)

Future is scheduling something that you both would be interested in doing for whatever reasons, sometime in the future. Something with value to both of you. YOU may want to have SEX with the girl right away in the future.. BUT SHE DOESN'T- not yet... She wants to get to know you a little better. So FUTURE is a way that she can get to know you a little better, before deciding if she wants to have a sexual

59

relationship with you or not. GIRLS LIKE THAT. And girls like guys who understand that.

YOU SEE the girl wouldn't go out on the first date with you if there weren't some possibility that she could have sex with you.

(BEING THERE is a subtle communication. She wouldn't be there if she wasn't somewhat interested.) So, unless you blow it, you will get sex eventually. HOWEVER, most guys DO blow it 9 out of 10 times instead of closing as I do 9 out of 10 times.

So how to create FUTURE? Well on a date it is relatively easy. APPLY what I have said above. ASK QUESTIONS and LISTEN. She will tell you something that gives you a subtle opportunity to see her again, and it should be something she would be really interested in and it won't scare her off.

EXAMPLE OF WHAT WORKS:

While you are listening she talks about the math class she is taking in college she is having trouble with. You happen to me a math genius. You simply say, "Well I am really good at math. If you would like

60

some help with your homework. Let me know." Then shut up. If she is interested in you, she will take the bait and say. "Yeah, oh I would so appreciate that" or something of the sort. If you have totally blown it by now and she doesn't want your help despite her learning disability, she won't take the bait. THAT WON'T HAPPEN unless you violated something else I have talked about here, and you talked about yourself too much, tried to be interesting, didn't listen, talked about sex or how pretty she was too much.

Another example is, while you are listening she says how she really likes to go dancing. So if you like dancing, you say, "Really? Me too. I love dancing, let's do that sometime." Or if you don't like to dance, don't lie. Say, "Really, then maybe you could help me because I don't know a thing about dancing but I think it's time I learned. Do you think you could teach me a little sometime?"

GET IT. Come up with something you guys could do in the future that she and you would really like to do, that's not a plea, "Can we go out again?"

By the way FUTURE is the key to meeting girls on the street, in the store, etc. Lots of girls will give you their phone numbers but about 90% of the beautiful women I know say they would never have a relationship with someone they met that way. BUT if you can establish FUTURE right there on the street or on the first call you can destroy those odds. And REMEMBER FUTURE is NOT "Can we go out sometime?" To a woman that just means you want sex, and you are asking for it before you have established any other value to her.

You see, meeting girls who work in stores or restaurants is easier than stopping them on the street, because the situation already has future built in....you know where they work, you can come back again and again, she can get to know you.... FUTURE you see.

But, stopping a girl on the street and establishing FUTURE. Now that can be a challenge! But, I've done it. Many times. You apply the same principles above. Don't talk about yourself. Be interested in her. Ask questions. Listen to the answers. When she says the opportune thing that you can tell has value to her, then jump right in with some FUTURE.

IN SUMMARY (AGAIN)

What I have given you here is an easy to implement, simple to understand SYSTEM that is guaranteed to get you results.

DATING without VOLUME of leads can be a lot more complicated than this.

Let me go back to the SALES analogy again.

VOLUME of LEADS is a salesman's most basic friend. If he can get a volume of leads most anyone can figure out what to do from there over time. Not everyone has equal closing ability. With a VOLUME of leads some guys may only close 1 out of 1000. Another may close 1 out of 100. Another may close 9 out of 10.

In the beginning, it doesn't matter what your "close" ratio is. Maybe it is 1 out of 1000. So use my techniques and generate 2500 phone numbers in a year and by the end of the year, with this scenario, you'll have 2.5 girlfriends. You see, VOLUME is workable no matter how bad you are.

Now for those guys who want to be PROS. Who want to learn how to be able to close 9 out 10 qualified women that they meet for a sexual relationship. YES you are going to have to learn a little more than what I have taught you here.

The techniques I have given you here are going to put you on the road to success. Some of you, once on the road, will figure everything out on your own. This is all you will ever need. Others will need additional help along the way to be ultimately able to close 9 out of 10 women that they meet. (Still others will have the ability to figure it out, but decide-- "Why bother, when someone else has already figured it out and is willing to tell me?")

That is why I have the book DATING TO RELATING – it goes into minute specifics and details and is the ultimate manual for guys who want to:

1) Take it to the next level and close 9 out of 10 qualified women that they meet.

2) Be able to pick up women in bars, in clubs, on the street.

3) Be able to seduce a woman—any woman, that has absolutely NO INTEREST in you.

4) To be able to make love to your woman like no other man Has ever done it.

5) To be able to meet and keep a hot woman that you are totally in love with for the rest of your life.

Yes, you can learn how to do all of these things, too.

But that is all for now.

Have fun guys!

Mr. L. Rx

P.S. I would love to hear about your success.

Email me at: <u>Success@DatingToRelating.com</u> and let me know.

ABOUT THE AUTHOR

Mr. L. Rx is the author of the Dating To Relating website (DatingToRelating.com), the author of the books "Dating To Relating – From A To Z", "How To Get Your Wife Or Girlfriend To Want More Sex" and the author of the original eReport "How I Got 700 Dates In One Year."

Mr. L. Rx has sometimes been called the "Observational Guru" rather than a "Dating Guru" as it is his ability to observe throughout his fifty plus years of experience that allows him to share dozens of unique dating and relationship strategies that apply to different personality types, different situations, and men and women of all ages.

http://www.DatingToRelating.com

Appendix A: Mr. L. Rx's Personal Online Dating Directory

Resources:

I've been asked to provide you with some resources – best places to set up on line accounts etc.

So here they are – (For most recent UPDATES Go to:)

http://datingtorelating.com/online_dating_sites__directories_and_reviews

The top two internet dating ad sites are:

1) **Craigslist.org** – best volume of responses but Craig's List has it quirks. They only let you put one ad in at a time for any category, and won't let you do multiple cities. When you first place an ad is when you get the most responses because it appears at the top of the category. However, craiglist.org will let you cancel your ad after three days or so and replace it. If you want to get maximum exposure that is the way to do it.

2) **Backpage.com** – for quality, my vote goes to backpage.com. I have gotten more dates from this publication than any other single source. Volume isn't as high per ad as craiglist.org, but they will let you place multiple ads per email address and they will let you pay for continuous listing and replacement to the top of the page every week. The quality of the girls responding also seems to be higher.

Now Here are the TOP 2 internet dating sites as judged by the guys visiting our site:

1) **Singlesnet.com** I guess guys not only like the fully functional FREE TRIAL OFFER but they like the site after trying it out too, because their feedback made this their number one favorite site- FREE TRIAL OFFER - NO CREDIT CARD REQUIRED.

2) **Metrodate.com** I guess guys liked this site too, because this was their number two selection- FREE TRIAL OFFER - Give it a try. Sign up for a free membership to create your own profile, visit the chat rooms, message boards, **dating tips** and more! Premium membership is also available! **Singles travel**, **singles events**, **nightlife** and **restaurant guides**, and much more!

DATING SERVICES -

OK so we are back to MY selections of the best sites to try.

1) MATCH.COM Well, in my book MATCH.COM.com is simply THE BIGGEST and THE BEST. If you want to meet a massive amount of dates you have to belong to Match.com. Now I just looked up my data from a typical year when I was using all these services and I saw that I got THREE TIMES as many women's phone numbers from MATCH.COM as the nearest competitor. (And 10 times the phone numbers I got from FRIENDFINDER which is number (2) below). For sheer numbers you can't beat MATCH.COM. Now Match.com is constantly changing and consequently does have its better and worse periods, but definitely give the free trial a whirl. In fact, you could do the 700 dates in one year (if you live in a big city or are willing to travel to one--from MATCH.COM alone.

2) FRIENDFINDERS.COM Now here is one of my old favorites. Now don't let what I said above tend to scare you away from using Friendfinder. All of these services are different and have their unique pluses and minuses. Women on here tend to be aggressive. Not as many hits as Match.com but the women tend to be more aggressive. SO I used FRIENDFINDER in a LAZY MAN's way. I never emailed anyone, I just sat back and let women email me. So yes I just got 1/10th the phone numbers, but I probably expended 1/20th the effort. Also a lot more international presence than match.com if you like that. Using BOTH Friendfinder and MATCH.COM provides you with a good balance of services.

3) LAVALIFE Another service that has been around a long time. It has some unique features and good response rates. Also has telephone based products, which I particularly liked and found to be more fun than the online stuff.

4) Mate 1 Online Dating - Mate 1 is another relatively new service that has a lot of aggressive women on it. Women are free - maybe that's why. But Give it a try. They usually have a free trial period for men.

5) FRIEND SEARCH is another relatively new service with a lot of COOL FEATURES and a HUGE INTERNATIONAL COMMUNITY. If you want to date INTERNATIONALLY give this one a try.

68

http://www.DatingToRelating.com

RELATIONSHIP SERVICES

These are MY Selections for Relationship Type sites

1) Perfectmatch.com - Now this is an interesting service. You can sign up and contact people for free. There is a 7 day free trial. Also have a very interesting profile match test that you should take.

2) True.com - This is a relatively new service but it's large and has pretty good action.

3) eharmony.com - This is one of the first sites on the RELATIONSHIP side of things. Another interesting site specializing in compatibility matching. Take the free personality test .

4) GREAT EXPECTATIONS - Well what can I say. They've been around for 30 years. Not really an on-line experience, but you can fill out your profile online for free. Give it a try if you are adventurous.

Appendix B: Other Books From Dating To Relating

How To Make Sex Last Longer - by Dr. Dating

Reg. Price: $20.00

Sale Price: $7.00

Save: $13.00

SPECIAL OFFER

DISCOVER AmericanExpress VISA [ ]   BUY NOW

PayPal
Add To Cart

View Cart

HOW TO MAKE SEX LAST LONGER   - $ 7.00

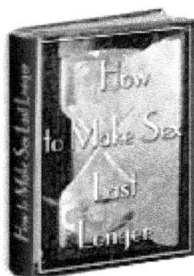

How To Make Sex Last Longer

** NEW 2007 Version **

Many sexually active males would like to "keep it up" longer - until their woman is fully satisfied and for their own more fulfilling, long lasting pleasure. Since it's no secret that it takes women longer to climax, guys need to delay their ejaculation if they really want to satisfy their partner. Everyone knows that longer intercourse is much more satisfying than "quickies" for both parties. Thanks to Dr. Dating, the secret is out - everyone can easily lengthen their lovemaking just by applying the techniques from Dr. Dating's latest eBook, *How to Make Sex Last Longer*.

70

http://www.DatingToRelating.com

Reg. Price: $20.00
Sale Price: $7.00
Save: $13.00

PayPal
Add To Cart

HOW TO GIVE ANY WOMAN ORGASMS - $7.00

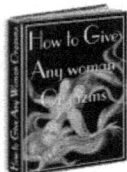

** NEW 2007 Version **

How To Give Any Woman Orgasms

The female body is a mystery to most men - even to those who have had thousands of sexual conquests. What is it that makes women tick? What do women really want in bed? These questions may have perplexed you for so long, and you're not alone. Finally, Dr. Dating has written a complete, tried and tested guide on *How to Give Any Woman Orgasms***.**

http://www.DatingToRelating.com

Reg. Price: $100.00
Sale Price: $14.00
Save: $86.00

NEW ARRIVAL   SPECIAL OFFER

DISCOVER   MasterCard   VISA   BUY NOW

PayPal
Add To Cart

SPECIAL OFFER!

Buy HOW TO MAKE SEX LAST LONGER and HOW TO GIVE ANY WOMAN ORGASMS - $14.00

and get THREE FREE compilation eBooks FROM Mr. L. Rx

EVERYTHING YOU WANTED TO KNOW ABOUT SEX POSITIONS

HOW TO BE A GREAT LOVER

HOW TO BE A GREAT KISSER

72

Reg. Price: $29.95
Sale Price: $19.95
Save: $10.00

NEW ARRIVAL

DISCOVER MasterCard VISA ▉ BUY NOW

HOW TO GET YOUR WIFE OR GIRLFRIEND TO WANT MORE SEX! - $19.95

PayPal
Add To Cart

How To Get Your Wife Or Girlfriend To Want More Sex

Women like sex just as much as men do. Any notion to the contrary is uneducated and inexperienced folly. Women probably do not "need" to have sex as frequently as men "need" to have sex, but, their like of and enjoyment of sex is as great if not greater than men's.

When a man is not getting as much sex as he would like in a relationship with a wife or girlfriend, he DEFINITELY is doing something wrong.

In this incisive and frank book, Mr. L. Rx outlines a program for men to eliminate their mistakes, and more importantly to increase the sexual desire from their wives and girlfriends.

Topics covered include what men do to "turn" women on and off, how to use "foreplay," "body language," "dress," and "romance" to create sexual interest in a woman your are in a relationship with, and a frank education in "sexual techniques" that will drive any woman wild and wanting maximum sex from you.

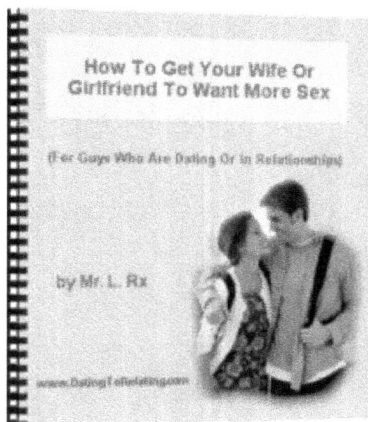

http://www.DatingToRelating.com

Reg. Price: $29.95
Sale Price: $19.95
Save: $10.00

NEW ARRIVAL

DISCOVER MasterCard VISA BUY NOW

THE KAMA SUTRA - EDITED BY MR. L. RX - $19.95

PayPal
Add To Cart

The Kama Sutra

The Kama Sutra is often thought of as the age old sex position manual. That is a common misconception. Only about 20% of the book concerns sex positions. In reality, The Kama Sutra is a comprehensive way of looking at all aspects of sexuality and sexual relationships. It is about getting to a place where you can maintain a good loving relationship, and where sex is about pleasing each other and knowing how to make each other feel good.

Written approximately 1500 years ago in India, this is the AGE OLD sex training manual and is a great book for anyone in a relationship. As an editor I have chosen the Sir Richard Burton translation of 1883. And I have tried to present to you what I think is an unmodified copy of that original translation. I have also tried to keep the text as original as I can - including spelling and punctuation. And although the original translation was not illustrated, I have researched and included fifty-nine 18thand 19th century Indian sex position illustrations to keep a certain amount of consistency with the writings.

74

Reg. Price: ~~$20.00~~
Sale Price: $7.00
Save: $13.00

SPECIAL OFFER

DISCOVER   MasterCard   VISA   [ ]   BUY NOW

PayPal
Add To Cart

HOW TO BE SUCCESSFUL WITH WOMEN - $7.00

** NEW 2007 Version **

How To Be Successful With Women

Ever thrown your arms up in the air, confused about something a woman said or did? You're not alone! Most men don't have an answer to the question of "What do women want?" Most men, that is, except for Dr. Dating. In his eBook "How to Be Successful with Women," Dr. Dating tackles the complexities of the female mind, and he's written it for YOU! He's handing you nothing short of the keys to the kingdom.

http://www.DatingToRelating.com

Reg. Price: ~~$20.00~~
Sale Price: $7.00
Save: $13.00

SPECIAL OFFER

DISCOVER   MasterCard   VISA   ▬   BUY NOW

PayPal
Add To Cart

THE ART OF CONVERSATION - $ 7.00

** Published 2006 **

The Art Of Conversation

We've all been there - the non-stop sweating and stuttering slowly becomes an embarrassment because you're simply too nervous to talk to the object of your attraction. Whether you're a sensitive guy or a sassy girl, you probably still get tongue-tied during parties, first dates, or even a simple conversation in your office lounge. Not to worry - Dr. Dating has created just the thing that can help you get your tongue out of a twist.

http://www.DatingToRelating.com

Reg. Price: $20.00
Sale Price: $7.00
Save: $13.00

SPECIAL OFFER

DISCOVER MasterCard VISA [ ] BUY NOW

PayPal
Add To Cart

THE BEGINNER'S GUIDE TO VIRTUAL SEX - $ 7.00

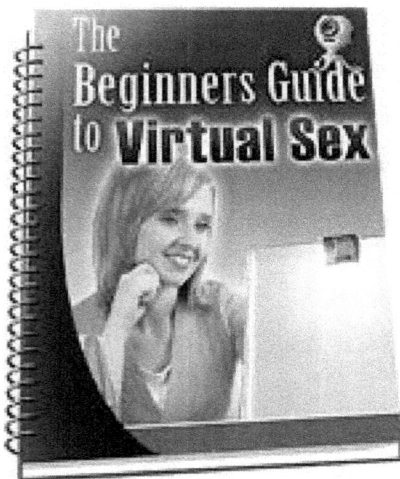

The Beginners Guide to Virtual Sex

It doesn't matter if you're a virgin or promiscuous, single or in a committed relationship - ABSOLUTELY ANYONE can have fulfilling, pleasurable sex in the virtual world. All you need is a phone line or an internet connection. This guide will show you EVERYTHING you need to know about mastering the world of virtual sex.

** Published 2007 **

Reg. Price: $20.00
Sale Price: $7.00
Save: $13.00

SPECIAL OFFER

DISCOVER MasterCard VISA [   ] BUY NOW

PayPal
Add To Cart

HOW TO FIND A F**K BUDDY - $7.00

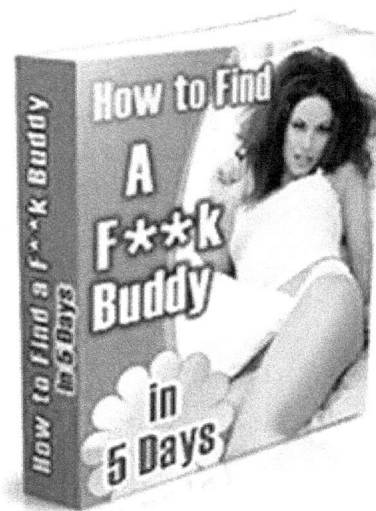

How To Find A Fk Buddy**

If you think it's impossible to list "sex" as a recreational activity, you're wrong! Whether you're as suave as James Bond or as ordinary as the Average Joe, you need to know the secrets of finding your own special "friend with benefits". Having a fk buddy can be a sensual adventure unlike any other and you deserve to be on that adventure! This guide can give you tried and tested methods that will help you get the f**k buddy**

** Published 2007 **

http://www.DatingToRelating.com

Reg. Price: $20.00
Sale Price: $7.00
Save: $13.00

SPECIAL OFFER

DISCOVER MasterCard VISA [ ] BUY NOW

PayPal
Add To Cart

COPING WITH A SMALL PENIS - $7.00

Coping With A Small Penis

This eBook is an inspiring story about how a young man copes with a small penis - and uses this "lack of size" as an advantage. It's no secret that most men worry about whether they are "big enough" to please a woman, and this story will definitely make you feel better about the size of your own penis, as well as your masculinity.

** NEW 2007 Version **

http://www.DatingToRelating.com

Reg. Price: ~~$20.00~~
Sale Price: $7.00
Save: $13.00

[SPECIAL OFFER]

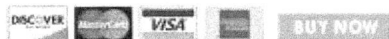 DISCOVER MasterCard VISA — BUY NOW

 PayPal
Add To Cart

DEALING WITH LONELINESS - $ 7.00

"Dealing With Loneliness"

By: SideKick

Dealing With Loneliness, while self explanatory, is one of the biggest problems for singles. This eBook is a quick and easy guide to tackling this problem and is a must read for all.

** Published 2007 **

http://www.DatingToRelating.com

Reg. Price: ~~$20.00~~
Sale Price: $7.00
Save: $13.00

PERSONALITY TYPES AND DATING GUIDE- $ 7.00

"Personality Quadrant's Dating Guide"

By: SideKick

Personality Quadrant's Dating Guide is a fun-filled, light-hearted guide on how to get a good date by understanding yourself as well as understanding and interpreting how your date will behave based on his or her personality type!

** Published 2007 **

http://www.DatingToRelating.com

Reg. Price: $20.00
Sale Price: $7.00
Save: $13.00

SPECIAL OFFER

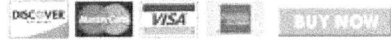

DISCOVER MasterCard VISA [ ] BUY NOW

PayPal
Add To Cart

GUIDE TO ADULT DATING - $ 7.00

Guide To Adult Dating

If you're tired of the normal dating routines of going out for coffee or dinner with someone you just met in a bar, you might want to try a *spicier* style of dating. Adult dating may just be the thing to kick your sex life into high gear. It's for anyone who wants to explore the extent of their sexuality, bring their fantasies to life, or try something new. With Dr. Dating's "Guide to Adult Dating", you can venture into the highly coveted world of sexy adult dates.

** Published 2006 **

http://www.DatingToRelating.com

Reg. Price: $20.00
Sale Price: $7.00
Save: $13.00

[SPECIAL OFFER]

DISCOVER MasterCard VISA   [ ]   BUY NOW

PayPal
Add To Cart

GREAT TIPS FOR DATING SUCCESS - $ 7.00

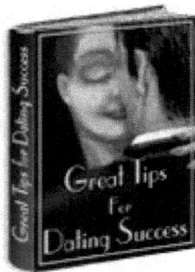

Great Tips For Dating Success

Whether you're looking for a fun, casual dating experience or a powerful romantic encounter, Dr. Dating's *Great Tips for Dating Success* is just the guide you need. This guide was written and researched by Dr. Dating himself, to help people from all walks of life to find and enjoy great dates. This eBook has all the hot tips and tricks that will help increase your dating success.

** NEW 2007 Version **

http://www.DatingToRelating.com

Reg. Price: $20.00
Sale Price: $7.00
Save: $13.00

SPECIAL OFFER

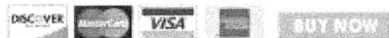

DISCOVER MasterCard VISA [ ] BUY NOW

PayPal
Add To Cart

5 STEPS TO ONLINE DATING SUCCESS - $ 7.00

5 Steps To Online Dating Success

By: SideKick

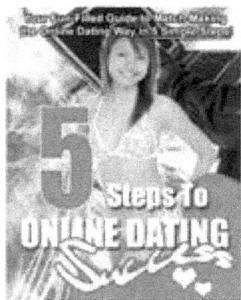

-What You Need to Know About Online Dating First!
-What Makes Online Dating So Different?
-Getting Started
-Making Yourself Look Like A Million Dollars

** Published 2007 **

http://www.DatingToRelating.com

Reg. Price: $20.00
Sale Price: $7.00
Save: $13.00

SPECIAL OFFER

DISCOVER MasterCard VISA BUY NOW

PayPal
Add To Cart

GUIDE TO ONLINE DATING - $ 7.00

** NEW 2007 Version **

Guide To Online Dating

Be honest - the single life can be depressing sometimes. You may try to find dates in bars, ask your friends to hook you up with someone, or even try dating services. If you don't' seem to have any success, you might find yourself giving up. But there's probably one dating frontier you haven't tried - online dating. More and more people all over the world are increasing their dating chances through the opportunities offered on the internet. With Dr. Dating's *Guide to Online Dating*, you can use the internet to give your dating life a complete makeover!

85

Reg. Price: ~~$20.00~~
Sale Price: $7.00
Save: $13.00

SPECIAL OFFER

DISCOVER MasterCard VISA [ ] BUY NOW

PayPal
Add To Cart

THE ULTIMATE MAN'S GUIDE TO ONLINE DATING - $ 7.00

The Ultimate Man's Guide to Online Dating

Ever feel like you're meeting the wrong women? Have you dated around and found that you're looking for something more casual while your date wants a marriage? Or do you simply get nervous in front of an attractive girl? Trust me, we've all been there. Sometimes we'd rather hang out with the guys and watch a football game rather than risk the frustration of going out with women you don't want to see again. There's a better world of women out there - and Dr. Dating has written the perfect dating guide for you!

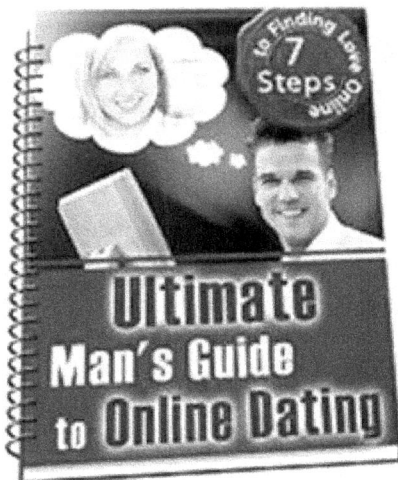

** Published 2007 **

85

http://www.DatingToRelating.com

Reg. Price: $20.00
Sale Price: $7.00
Save: $13.00

SUCCESSFUL ONLINE DATING - UK EDITION - $7.00

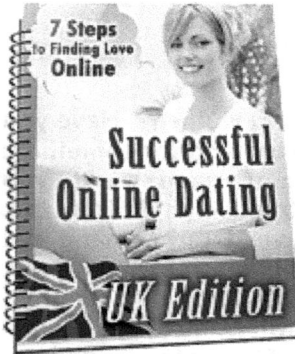

Successful Online Dating - UK Edition

Face it, mate - the dating world can be scary. When you think about dating, you think about the stress, rejection, and anxiety that comes with it. Why even date at all? The good news is that ONLINE DATING has changed all this. We now live in a world where we can collect and select potential dates without the grueling experiences of real world dating. By the time you actually meet an online date in person, you're ready for it! You know who you're dealing with. You know you won't face rejection ever again.

** Published 2007 **

http://www.DatingToRelating.com

Reg. Price: $20.00
Sale Price: $7.00
Save: $13.00

SPECIAL OFFER

DISCOVER MasterCard VISA ▭ BUY NOW

PayPal
Add To Cart

A TEENAGER'S GUIDE TO DATING - $ 7.00

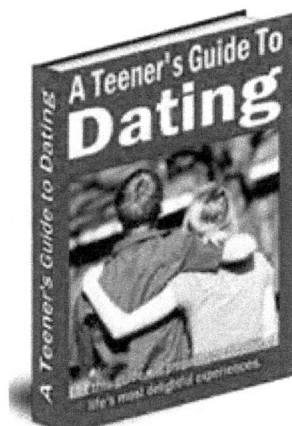

"A Teenager's Guide To Dating"

By: SideKick

This is a comprehensive 128 page eBook written for Teenagers and the Adults who care about them. This eBook covers every aspect of teenage dating. A must for Teenagers and their Parents alike.

** Published 2007 **

http://www.DatingToRelating.com

Reg. Price: ~~$20.00~~
Sale Price: $7.00
Save: $13.00

SPECIAL OFFER

DISCOVER   MasterCard   VISA   ☐   BUY NOW

PayPal
Add To Cart

SUCCESSFUL DATING FOR WOMEN - $ 7.00

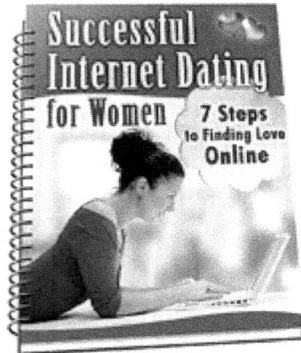

Successful Internet Dating For Women

Ever feel like you're *never* going to find the man of your dreams? Have you dated around and found most of your dates frustrating and disappointing? Trust me, girl, we've all been there. Sometimes we'd rather sit on the couch, eat some ice cream, and watch the latest John Cusack movie. *There has to be a better life than this, right?* Well, there is! We've got the ultimate dating guide to help you find Mr. Right!

** Published 2007 **

http://www.DatingToRelating.com

Dating To Relating - From A To Z - $39.95

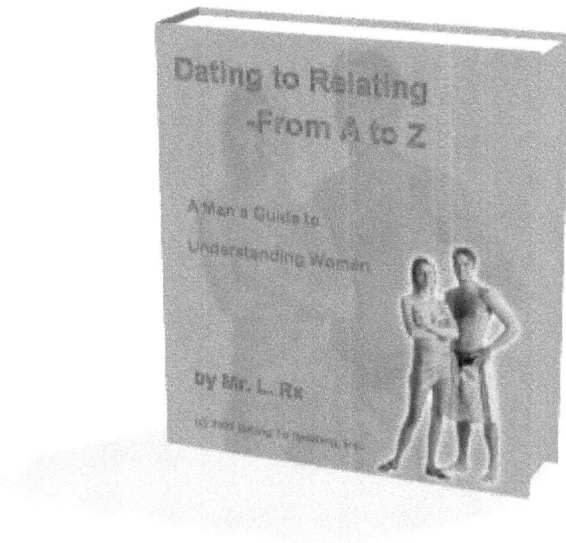

Dating To Relating - The Book

Price:$39.95

Dating to Relating - from A to Z (A man's guide to Understanding women)

"How I went from Stupid to Smart in just 50 years" or

"How and Why I got more dates with, relationships with and proposals from Hot Young Women at age 50 than I did at age 25.

http://www.DatingToRelating.com

www.ingramcontent.com/pod-product-compliance
Lightning Source LLC
Chambersburg PA
CBHW081159270326
41930CB00014B/3223